To kell

Wanderer

CONCEPT Meera Chowdhry | ART Niloufer Wadia | FOREWORD P C K Prem
POETRY ❈ Rajender Krishan

1

Complimentary
Copy

Wanderer
By
Rajender Krishan Chowdhry

Setu Publications
* Pittsburgh, PA (USA) *
© Rajender Krishan Chowdhry,
NY 11364, USA; rk@boloji.net

All illustrations in this book
© Niloufer Wadia, Pune, India.

We would be pleased to receive email correspondence regarding this publication or related topics at setuedit@gmail.com.

ISBN-13 (paperback): 978-1-947403-15-4

Distributed to the book trade worldwide by Setu Publications, USA

Setu Literary Publications, Pittsburgh, USA

To Meera Chowdhry, my wife,
for being with me:

nudging, objecting, coaxing, guiding,
and yet sanctifying all my wanderings,
to introspect, cognize and grow together
to accept and face Life, fearlessly,
as it unfolds,
with humility, gratitude and resilience.

About the Book

If a man knows roots and feels obliged, well, it has meaning or else it is a huge charade. To maintain concord in relations is must. Cordiality brings warmth and purpose. To live with a difference is a sign of harmony, is the advisory message. Here, psychotherapy in lyrics is genuine, experiential and born of impressions and so these determine the language but, in such annotations, he seems careful and so, he often changes the lyrical track from the philosophic to the more *bona fide* facets of life. It is movement to near perfection if a man understands how to celebrate it excellently and perceptively.

Contents

List of Poems

Foreword

I am amazed when I try to figure out the hiatus between the actuality and philosophic perspective the poet in Rajender Krishan presents in *Wanderer*. The poet, at times, expresses a thought tersely as if an adage or a proverb. If one concentrates, it conveys multiple meanings. Just look at the beauty and essence of some truisms.

The wandering mystic
gives a discourse on death
to explain the value of life (Discourse) or

"the meditating mystic /experiences /a soothing melody/on feeling silence (Tranquility) or - The wandering mystic,/pensively enters in the/ ashes of burnt memories (Fragrance) or No wonder, the mystic meditates/ tranquil with dropped eyelids/ oblivious to the transient spectacle (View)."

These are just a few illustrations of intellectual range, the poet reveals. It is a huge leap from *Solitude* to *Amma's Gospel to Wonderer*.

To comprehend the mystery of birth, death and rebirth is a riddle and let it play the game and it shall keep interest in life, for no one knows what future holds for man and thus, cyclic pattern holds many a secret concealed in womb, which is forever 'inexpressible.'

Let it keep mesmerizing
mystifying and overwhelming
It is fun to play hide-and-seek.

He confirms that a man looks out for the eternal – an amorphous image. However, a wandering man ends nowhere. A transient manifestation enthralls always, for identification with the body it is that causes enticement and ultimate end. So is the life -

Is it plausible that the chaos caused,
due to the combination of elements,
the *gunas*, nature and the principles
of Life at large, is what manifests
camouflaged as the mind?

'Mind' is normally undisciplined and stays out of control as contrasting perceptions crowd even while efforts to find clarity continue. To extract 'the self' from the chaotic situation is required to organize life's anxieties and solutions, only then one obtains correctness in life. 'Conscience' is 'the real self' sans dualities but mind remains unsteady and needs restraint so tell scriptures, but it proves a mirage, an understanding dawns, he deliberates to find a coherent meaning but feels puzzled.

Understand, 'Shadows' teaches eternal lessons of life if a man understands properly, and it is approaching surrealistic areas where to touch truth is a dilemma, he suggests and thus, he moves from one side to another but hangs about, as predicament in life and existence persists. A subtle movement from one thought to another leads to the configuration of 'opinion' that stays to express protrusions, perceptions and experiences, some complex, a few mystifying and some inconceivable, he makes it clear and tells man to single out the right approach.

Poet's observations are remarkable, and it is possible only if one experiences what one says in words. It turns authentic and reliable. Again, he comes back to the vagaries of mind - wicked at one moment and saintly next minute, and that is precisely the situation when one's pains, joys and pleasures whether momentary or long-term create bondages even while man tries to pull out 'the self' from the vortex of uncertainties that life is. RK leads you to different thoughts born of faith rooted in personal terrain and so with it, he expands the vision to encompass the whole universe and that way, he tries to connect man to universal fraternity of compound thoughts in search of an ideal foothold to organize life's dilemma. Such insoluble challenges pierce deep into the poet's conscience and this, he relates to life's gamut extensively.

Density of thoughts chases the poet in 'Creativity', where he endeavors to arrive at the logical cosmic vision that is anarchy in perfect order, a duality amidst multiple choices of thought patterns, which is a real mystery. Questions on sources of manifestations and dispositions arise to befuddle as true expression eludes, again a product of mind in a state of tsunami. Such a condition defies transparency despite efforts, for it is to find faultless linkage in inadequate reconciliation of diverse thoughts.

It is unfolding of the subtle, the gross and the transcendent elements, and a run into the amorphous, the infinite and the endless, one wants to understand.

Having experienced such a
transcendence, the poet
aiming to articulate the infinite,
ends up embracing duality,
to give birth to poetry.

Life has its own constraints of movement and carries its attributes elusively. A man should wake up and comprehend it and positively grasp the depth of realities, the poet wishes to convey in 'Crux' and 'Insight'.

Life presents varied forms in the shape of words and names and it is an entrance to comprehend its multiple facets (Crux) with the deluding syntax.

Love or hate; Life has a universal trait
Each is the maker of one's personal fate.

Life steadily occupies the innermost stage of anxieties as intellectuals continue to 'Debate' infinitely sans finality, though a sense of established superiority overwhelms and so it descends down to ridiculous situation. Here, obtuse argument takes over and defies logical finale but a wise one just takes notice of ego and ethical undertones -

paying total attention, not to the orators,
but to the words, and walked away content,
akin to the wandering mystic,
with the discovery of an aphorism.

It is a wish of a poet to carry on efforts to explore new pastures to obtain fulfillment in life in uncertain and thorny times where the journey will be enigmatic, and the co-traveler will be equally a stranger, unknown where if a man is true, life is meaningful,

… walk and wander with me
on the new voyage, instead
I pray, keep me blessed
to be true to myself (Wanderer)

Elsewhere he says,

Was the wanderer ever tied
with instructions this way?

15

Bondage free then and even now
he treads carefree all the way (Carefree)

While on a journey, if you stumble upon a stone remove it so that others do not fall…a great virtue it is and so he affirms in 'Consider.' 'Schooling' teaches art of life…how to walk, negotiate, reconcile, challenge and yet modestly bow to grace while 'Learning-matters' conveys duties of a disciple and a preceptor where sincerity and truth are the cardinal principles, he states modestly.

Knowing change as
the eternal law of nature
To act in harmony with existence.

Life is a great teacher. Doubts teach man to meditate deeply and one learns life's mysteries as it wishes to teach and be sure that 'Life teaches/ in her own/mysterious ways. / No one is spared (Learning)'. Karma, Duty, Viewpoint and Cheats are little lyrics like many others that end on advisory notes and appeal. It is good to restrain enticements or temptations in life, which are signs of guarantee and distinction whereas greed and nasty thoughts lead to self-destructive acts and prove burdensome, so he avers in 'Contrast' and 'Attitude' that determine that cautious inclines coerce life to victory.

React not inanely
to make the situation dire
resiliently respond,
the mess will appear minor.

Harmony is amiable to recognition and admiration and grants one another a space adequate to grow in life notwithstanding its proclivities towards frequent multiplicity in outlook and approach to life.

Cognizing perpetually
that *Life*, though forever in a flux,
is simply dynamic and wonderful,
united in its existential diversity (Accord)

Relations are important in life, yet the degree ought to be underlined or else flaws create awesome and lethal situations when one recalls relations, he opines. One is selfish 'Remembrance' conveys. Obligations towards parents are *dharma* of a man, a voyage to locate one's origin, an indefinable exploration.

However, hope strengthens life, and each 'Dawn' brings inner illumination as it wakes up to life of essence and revitalizes hope while love grants extra energy, a man ought to understand.

the vision of light
and the womb of silence

invigorated with her tender kiss
begins the sound of music.

Providence assigns the work of creation to the womb –to the mother where the seed finds eternal refuge and then, re-germinates. It symbolizes the grandeur of cycle of ageless transformation.

As the tree of life
though seemingly whole
I silently persist
in clinging to earth
for sustenance and power
to realize the eternal glory
of the cycle of changing seasons. (Tree of Life)

However, the eternal master knows but not the fanatic or a crazy enthusiast, who is excited but appears cut off from reality. A man speaks of the fundamental truth when he talks of the design of great master, who gives shape to each creation in an impeccable way. One has to play his role forgetting identity. Let the character he plays be his God on his side and so he will do immaculately well.

Life is a play
so the masters say
everyone is given
a role to portray… (Flawless)

Treatment of certain thoughts, attitudes and qualities of man in a few poetic portrayals simply astounds. Attitude is how one maintains inner and outer equilibrium despite provocation. Inane reaction can be hazardous if man is able to expunge dark regions of demeanor and guarantees exclusion. In identical element of wisdom, he epigrammatically describes the true meaning of 'Guilt, Greed and Ponder.' Attitude of contemporary life is strange rather preposterous where oddities get recognition (Venal). Cheats and swindlers swell like the 'Corona' wave where not only social ethos is indistinct and cloaked but also particularize treacherous times.

The deadly wave of *Corona*
seems to be aggressively distorting
social ethos and the worldview;
times are really getting tough.

Pondering over the proliferation (Syndrome?) of 'marvels of medical technology…and capsules and overabundance of treatment results in total futility where 'the fight to remain alive itself /is becoming a novel ailment' and therefore, an ironic tragedy of times it is. The poet is blunt and thus, underlines failure of the system and here, perhaps the mysterious 'Corona' and its variants are sneaking into life to disconcert already unsystematic living styles of contemporary man and thus, he makes a radical departure from customary suggestions of optimism.

Interestingly, most of the short lyrics are philosophic, and signal intensity of condensed thought progression where one ought to wield hard to reach what message it contains. If a man gets rid of the truth of 'Thine' and 'Mine' it leads to life's quintessence, for in duality only bewilderment and synthesis survive and puzzle flouting ethical tenor. Duality drives to conflict, as 'I, Mine and thine' are sources of ego, pride, contradictions and confrontations, abuse, arrogance and ultimate collapse of dignity but continuity in existence.

Over the eons,
biased and strategic
disputes over
u*s* and *them*;
mine and *thine*,
have caused
crusading wars
allowing the mafia (Elementary and Exploitation)

A man changes into a subtle operator in life (Approach). Mind is a field where contradictory forces continue to create disarray but through rationalization, one can scrutinize various probabilities to subdue inessential components to arrive at the right conclusion where the real and genuine propensities turn quite perceptible.

one must
earnestly pursue skillfully;
as excellence manifests in one
who is true to self than trying
to imitate or engage in a rat race.

A correct choice of path is good for achieving the objective in life and the work should be rewarding and fulfilling and not an empty drumbeating to get rid of 'routines', for these transform lives into a multipart impasse where it requires appropriate sorting out. He makes a grippingly innocuous philosophic observation on life.

Prayers are answered
Only if you know
why to pray
how to pray.

Through love a man can realize the 'the self' and it is sole objective of human life and so one ought to be true to oneself, is gist of 'Commonsense' where with proper 'Management' of time and working with total 'self-discipline' one attains the goal. A man should understand that an undignified life takes a man nowhere and pushes him to 'self-destruction' and therefore, only life of meaning grants it substance and recognition.

'Dawn' offers glimpses of hopes and illumination as sound of music brings consciousness to a life of sleep and inactivity that bestows deliverance. It also signals unity of variations as beating of celestial drum brings about synthesis in frenzied voices.

Unperturbed, the Master
paints the canvas
unifying diversity
and beating His drum
in the union of rhythms
orchestrates, the dance of the universe.

When the poet speaks of 'the dance of the universe' it is probably 'the cosmic dance of lord *Shiva* that signifies joyful interaction and stream of the dynamic and stationary divine energy one may find inherent in the principle of creation, preservation and destruction.

Interestingly, many a time, his lyrics appear interlinked to convey a consolidated meaning. 'Desire' is in fact, 'fire of life' that chases man throughout and finally, a union is the final note of conciliation resulting in 'marriage' as 'awaking together gratified, / until the final curtain is drawn' and the reward is the union of bodies, minds and hearts if properly understood. Otherwise, fissures in 'compatibility' threaten.

'Serenity' is blissful where one ought to discipline waywardness of body, mind and heart to live in a tranquil state of mind - serenity. Serenity is restraining '…the conflicting mind/face squarely life's daily grind/with courage, resilience, and grace/disallowing mystic *Serenity* to efface.' 'Togetherness' is extension of private harmony to universal experience as efforts to explore 'the self' continue to attain new meaning of objective. The spirit of life beyond bodily perception (here, the poet relives realization of marital joy) provides eternal bliss and therefore, delving deep into the 'sanctity' of relations is a path to understanding 'awareness - a transient trivia?' as he arrives at a conclusion in 'cognition', a true insight.

P C K Prem
January 7, 2021

Acknowledgements

Wanderer would not have ever materialized without the support of my beloved wife for 45 years, **Meera Chowdhry** – an alumnus of Miranda College, who has always been the first to read and reflect to whatever gets written by me. She is a pillar of strength rendering much need support to everyone in the family. She is also my constant companion and support, physically, mentally and spiritually in all my wanderings. While agreeing on some and differing on others in a healthy way, she believes and *lives* the famous marital saying, "Until death does us apart".

My gratitude to **Mr. P C K Prem** for writing the foreword to this book. Prem ji (P C Katoch of Garh-malkher, Palampur, HP, a former academician, civil servant and member of Himachal Public Service Commission, Shimla), a triangular author of several books and a post-graduate (1970) in English literature from Punjab University, Chandigarh, is a poet, novelist, short story writer, translator and a critic in English from Himachal Pradesh.

**Niloufer Wadia** who has interpreted each and every poem in this book with illustrations, after having spent over 20 years in advertising, quit to follow her first loves, fine art and illustration. She paints in acrylics and watercolors, and illustrates in a wide variety of styles, from children's picture books to medical tomes, in the traditional and digital media.

My sincere thanks to Dr. Jaipal Singh, Prof. Jaydeep Sarangi, Dr. Sulakshna Sharma, Neera Pradhan, Prof. Shubha Tiwari, Mandira Ghosh, Rajiv Khandelwal, Giti Tyagi, G. Swaminathan, Prof. R.K. Bhushan Sabharwal, Prof. Dr. Nar Deo Sharma and Hema Ravi, for previewing Wanderer. The previews are appended at the end of the book.

Above all I cannot help but express my gratefulness to all those known and unknown people, natural elements, environment, seasons and my own moods, that consistently wander with me, nudging, coaxing, guiding to introspect, cognize and learn to accept and face *Life, as it unfolds*, with humility, gratitude and resilience.

Rajender Krishan
January 7, 2021

Preface

The mind oscillates between turmoil and calm, at times for no rhyme and reason and the thoughts seem to go nowhere or merely hover aimlessly, the wandering begins to search a purpose, to understand the cause and to ascertain the destination.

The anxieties caused by the tragedies, trauma and commotion during the pandemic of 2020 compelled almost everyone to ponder and attempt to reign the wild horses galloping in the mind's racecourse. The pandemic also forced everyone in some degree or the other to use restrain, introspection and prayers to regain hope and courage to overcome the tsunami of fear. Each one dealt and is dealing with the situation in one's own best way.

Wanderer covers poems that have their genesis in the same environment with a churning of fleeting thoughts and are an attempt to find answers to uncertainties and the complex questions arising therefrom.

Rajender Krishan
December 16, 2020

Inexpressible

That what is inexpressible
is best to remain nestled
as the eternal witness

Let it keep mesmerizing
mystifying and overwhelming
It is fun to play hide-and-seek

In this wonderful play
of cyclic life, should it even matter
who finds whom, next?

View

That what is formless
is yet the only eternal form
Searching which

the anxious wanderer
walks with protruding eyes
while the formless rests within

No wonder, the mystic meditates
tranquil with dropped eyelids
oblivious to the transient spectacle

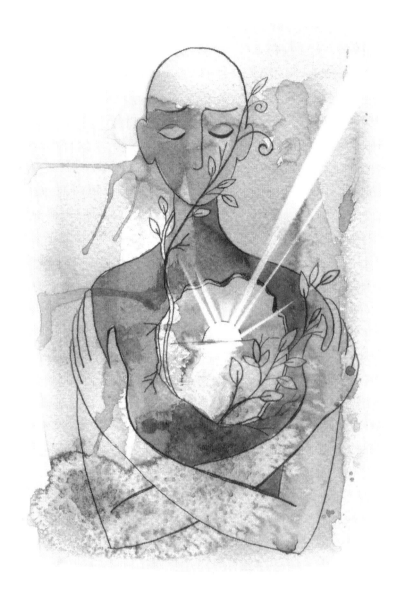

Remembrance

One searches
what is lost
One tries to remember
what is forgotten

But how does one
even reminiscence about
the parent, who has
long been gone
and yet *is* a part
of one's very own being?

Cordial

You write, I recite
You compose, I describe
You decide, I abide

It is so comfortable
to live together, in harmony,
with all these differences

Cheers!

Mother

Image the One
nestled within
one's very being
as the mother;
always caring
eternally vigilant
and guiding
with her s*utras*
of integrity

Not listening to
this sacred voice
or suppressing it
is self-deception,
being delusional,
and disrespectful
to the Creator

Mind

It seems that the mind
is wired to be a part of
the grand cosmic network
which causes it to stay fraught
with opposing perspectives!

No wonder, every idea,
appears to accompany
with doubt or conviction,
hesitancy or inclination,
forming a constant tussle.

From where else do emerge
the *personal* likes and dislikes,
pull and push of strange influences,
leading to a conflict of nerves,
causing hasty or indolent reactions?

Is it plausible that the chaos caused,
due to the combination of elements,
the *gunas*, nature and the principles
of Life at large, is what manifests
camouflaged as the mind?

Conscience

Conscience, the *apparent* Self,
transcends all dualities,
is poised, a carefree witness,
knows all, yet remains buried
beneath the vagaries of mind.

This sense of right and wrong
pokes, nudges through whispers
indicating the do's and don'ts
reasoning why and what to do
but stays reserved on *how* to act.

The scriptures have since eons
preached to conquer the mind,
to crush the *reservation on how*
for a logical and ethical response
rather than a reckless reaction.

Any doubts?

Shadows

Expanding and shrinking
always accompanying
is one's own shadow,
the dogged companion

A natural *aide-memoire*,
reminds about the brilliance
of the Sun within,
as one's own conscience.

The *joie de vivre*,
stimulating and prodding,
whispers right counsel
on every step one takes

Listening, the dutiful heeds
and principles become alive
Ignorant muzzles the whisper
thus leads a fraudulent life

One wonders if there is a need
for anyone else to guide?

Opinion

Everything is essentially
a mere projection
of one's perception;
the opposing experiences
of pain, pleasure
profits, losses
are but ephemeral,
a transient reality

Yet it is due to
our clinging bondage
with either the cause or the effect
that makes our mental makeup
as our enemy or a friend

One wonders, if
there is a power on earth
stronger than one's own mind
that can give blissful joy
or is there another devil
that can give pain worse than
what gets inflicted
from the enemy within?

Creativity

One recognizes in all humility,
the difficulty of true expression,
when acknowledging everything
to be for a reason in the cosmic
diversity, as impeccably perfect
beautiful, exotic, delicate, erotic,
effulgent in its own brilliance,
that only becomes restless upon
contact with something unusual,
rather, attractively wonderful.

Such a link causes various
manifestations, depicting
all kind of moods, grasping
which begins the genesis of
fresh desires of novel ingenuity.

The invigorated poet dives in
the ocean of fantasy to reach
its very depths to witness
the unfolding of the marvel,
from one form to another
changing from grosser
to subtler to sublime layers;

briefly, comes face to face
with what is the formless,
limitless and endless.

Having experienced such a
transcendence, the poet
aiming to articulate the infinite,
ends up embracing duality,
to give birth to poetry.

Crux

Every form has a name
Every name is a word
Two together create a fusion
One alone creates confusion

The word may be dust or gold
Focus and it begins to unfold

Information layered in each word
Is discovered by how it is uttered
Every word is a wondrous story
Name reveals its nature in glory

What perception ably does one hold?
Experience or the one that was told!

Inferences are harbingers of desire
Causing action to acquire and require
Fear of loss breeds the habit of greed
Gluttonous ego sows a personal seed

Sown individuality blooms from the root
Destiny calls to reap the bitter-sweet fruit

Recognize everything that conspires
Why the prize and penalty transpire
With aspirations that one proceeds
Intention impels how one deals

Love or hate; Life has a universal trait
Each is the maker of one's personal fate

51

Insight

Life is a play
the world a stage
and we all actors
so affirm the seers

Yet, notwithstanding
this knowledge,
one is captivated
by *her* wonders

Enamored, it matters not
if the glass is raised
as a tribute to
the rains of pleasure

Or drowned agonizingly
in the floods of sorrow
Lamenting on the pain
there is surely no gain

Fascinating it may be
being lost in denial
but meaningful it is to
bravely fight the battle

In this elusive drama
one needs to awaken,
at least once, and
truly grasp the script

To be alive sanguinely
and witness the reality
in the marvelous act of
the ultimate scene

~*~

Everyone's encounter,
distinctively unique
Curtains drawn
Script unchanged.

55

Flawless

Life is a play
so the masters say
everyone is given
a role to portray

So be the performer
understand the scenes
follow instructions
given by the director

Get not attached
to the character
when curtain draws
erase the actor

Retrace yourself to
the untainted carefree
neither this nor that
no artiste, no act

Whodunit

Meditating together,
both aspired to transcend
the mundane and
attain harmony

Yet, being impressionists
they could not help but
kept screaming at each other
to remain silent ...

Deafened by the commotion
they are now unable to hear
the celestial song of tranquility
in the theater of war within

... the perpetual inquiry
of whodunit continues ...
while the unperturbed mystic
witnesses the chaotic drama

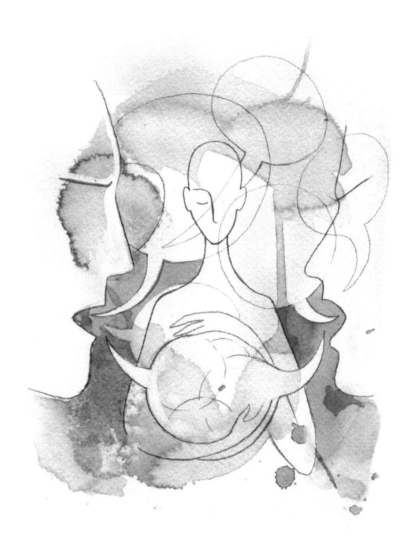

Debate

Two renowned scholars
were discussing the fundamentals of life
giving excellent speeches;
the audience was cheering them
with applause and the sound of the claps
differentiated who was leading.

That's when the sensible discussion
transformed into a competition,
inviting *Ego* and tossing *Morality*
out of the window. The idea of winning
turned the discussion into an obtuse argument
and the original idea was pulverized.

The debate ended inconclusive.
However, there was one observer,
paying total attention, not to the orators,
but to the words, and walked away content,
akin to the wandering mystic,
with the discovery of an aphorism.

Transformation

Went to the temple
to get some peace
Came back lugging
the tightened identity
of a burdened typecast

Bumped into a mystic
discussed a prosaic idea
Returned home
with a fractured ego
but a liberated Self

Wonderful

Having discarded
the egoistic albatross,
the mystic unknown
wanders carefree

Venerating the present
with every step taken
humming blissfully
the song of liberation

Discourse

Meeting a tense crowd
grief stricken and
emotionally disturbed

The wandering mystic
gives a discourse on death
to explain the value of life

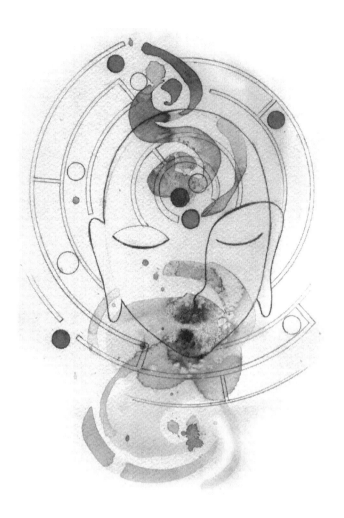

Cipher

Meditative mystic
wants to remember
by unlearning
what was learnt

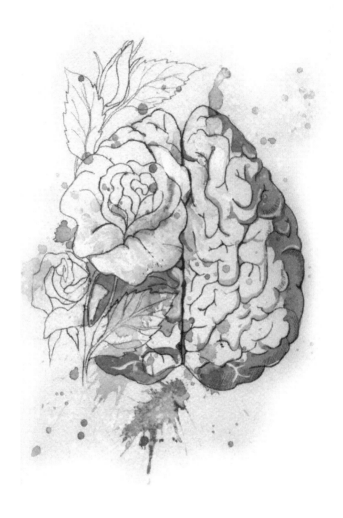

Ennui

On being questioned
if he was ever bored,
the wandering mystic
referred to boredom

as a product of one's
incompetence to be calm
while being creatively
engaged, doing nothing

Matchless

In the rat race, when
each one is trying to
outdo everyone else,
wanting to be the best

The wandering mystic
continues to bask
in the pristine glory
of his unique Self

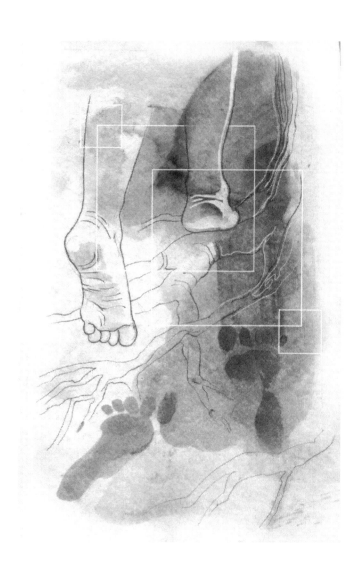

Fulfilment

The mystic - drowned
in his wandering self,
leaves marks of footsteps
as expressions of fulfilment
on a known journey
with no beginning or end.

Tranquility

In gratitude and
absolute surrender
the meditating mystic
experiences
a soothing melody
on feeling silence

Veracity

Denying and defying
ensnaring temptations,
the mystic warrior
wisely disciplined

Content and caring
remains virtuous,
aware of being eyed
by the watchful Self

Outlook

Resolute to live
in poverty of fear
the mystic warrior
learns to treasure

Wealth of strength
and pearls of wisdom
becoming self-reliant
to defend principles

Contentment

On a simple exchange
with disgruntled crowd
the wandering mystic

> Chose renunciation
> to feel relaxed, instead of
> getting agitated by denunciation

> Urged forbearance
> and patience, instead of
> wickedness and anger

> Suggested goodwill and
> harmony, in place of
> venom of hate and envy

Accepted all as they were
and moved on, blissfully
sharing the essence of love

Fragrance

Contemplating on
the aroma emanating
from snipped flowers

The wandering mystic,
pensively enters in the
ashes of burnt memories

Breathes transient distress
of separation, felt while
seeking the venerated Self

and the wandering continues

Sly

When mind wanders elsewhere
insincere becomes the prayer,
Blame not the chosen deity
that ignores the phony piety

      Ready to kill and destroy
      in the name of the unknown,
      Unwilling to bend even a bit
      to render help to downtrodden

Advising everyone of good action
flowered with expressive speech,
Talk not of doctrines or morality
if practicing not, what you preach

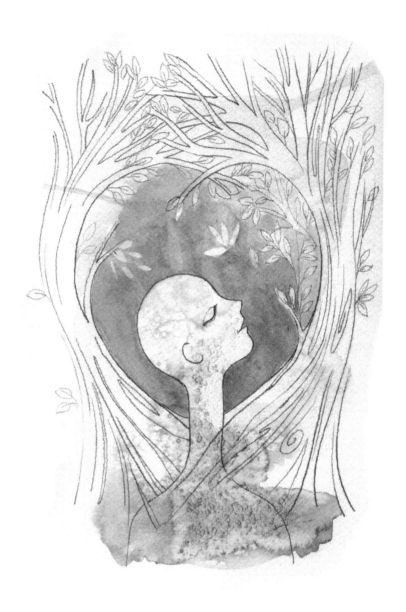

Reverence

When one is aware
of being in the lap
of Mother Earth
one feels blessed.

The search ceases
as the wanderings impart
experience and wisdom
to cognize everything

On the path, being
placed by events and
circumstances, for
a purpose

Thus, I bow in reverence
to anything that brings
my journey closer
to the Unknown.

Wanderer

Times are uncertain
Life unpredictable
yet, desires abound
Seeking fulfillment

Allow me to exert
for one more day
in my attempt to empty
the trunk of cravings

The new journey
must begin, unsullied,
without any luggage,
to explore the unknown

Verily all will belong
to the same Cosmos
yet, let me not wonder
as to who will meet

walk and wander with me
on the new voyage, instead
I pray, keep me blessed
to be true to myself

Consider

Imagine while walking
a stone on the way
makes one stumble

Know the stone to be
the providential ploy,
for one to be *found*

If the mis-stepped fall
becomes meditative
to arouse compassion

The stone would be
moved aside, preventing
others from tripping

Making one fulfilled
by doing a small thing
gently in a big way

Though the unwise,
kicking and hurting more,
will limp on, mindlessly

Schooling

Life taught me, incredibly young,
through accidents and design,
how-to walk, in sync with *her*

Making me accept situations
eventfully forcing my assent to
her surprisingly changing routes

Her simply tough tutoring
in the School of Challenges
began lessons with gratitude

Followed by aptitude, fortitude,
encouraging to aim for altitude
smiling with a caring attitude

The syllabus covered:
Acceptance of ephemeral,
inexorable and the irreversible

Knowing change as
the eternal law of nature
To act in harmony with existence

Seeking to be courageously ethical
Being not ashamed to question
Crossing all hurdles to gain insight

Having a sincere purpose in pursuits
Being morally gratified of actions
Having humility to respect my mentors

~*~

The walk with *her* has been
exciting, fulfilling and blissful
And now in my twilight,

She gracefully prepares me
to be ready for a new latitude
in the singularity of *her* solitude

Learning Matters

Teacher

A principled mentor
is the one, who knows
the subject to be taught,
yet again, thoroughly prepares,
for proficient transmission

Gauging simultaneously
that the lessons taught are
being received mindfully
by the students for
precise assimilation.

Student

Transforming the learning
into knowledge and wisdom
and to skillfully apply in
their work-a-day life, is the
challenging onus of the pupils

Successful achievement
by an apprentice is the
reverent and profound response
to the trainer, who celebrates
in ecstasy for the job well-done.

Learning

When in doubt
worry not. It compels,
one to translate,
contemplate, meditate

Soon enough
a spark ascends
to ignite and engulf,
one in an inferno

Bringing to the brink
it offers no options,
but to learn and
discover the answer

Life teaches
in her own
mysterious ways.
No one is spared.

Elementary

The elements five
Performed a Yoga
And built the temple divine

The mundane *"I"*
A mere guest
Forgot its primordial shine

Trapped and deluded
It struggles to discover
The Truth of *"Thine"* and *"Mine"*

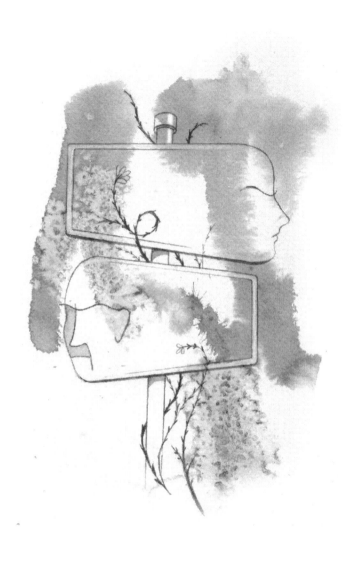

Exploitation

Difference between
isms is not due to
the universality of
the Laws of Physics
or the Principle - Truth,
but due to the control of
vested interests and
time, space, causation

Over the eons,
biased and strategic
disputes over
u*s* and *them*;
mine and *thine*,
have caused
crusading wars
allowing the mafia

to loot and plunder,
generating vast fiefdoms
by wrecking the masses
here, there, everywhere

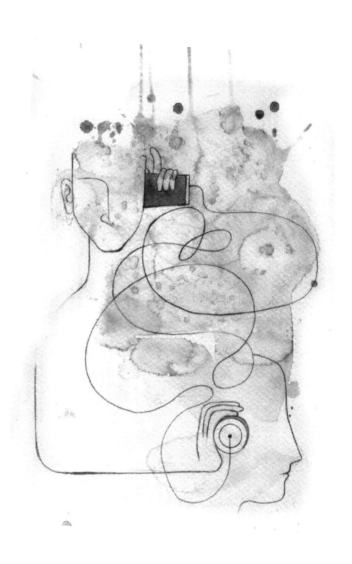

Presumptions

Not hearing from someone
dear and known for a long time
does not authorize me to

Enter imaginations and conclude
that the fellow has taken the ferry
on a journey to the world beyond.

What if, I did not happen to be
on the list of the survivors?
If I did not suppose too much

I could have perhaps used any of
the available tools to connect.
What prevented?

Who wanted to script the play
of being attached or detached
in an inter-connected world?

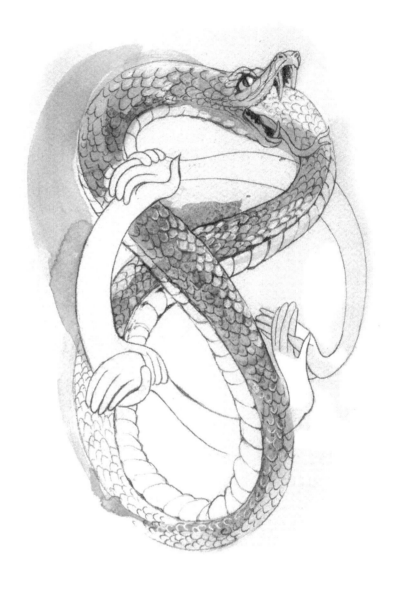

Karma

The *Karmic* principle
is indeed, candid, and blunt
Whichever way one deals
it rebounds with equal brunt

Fair and square transactions
garner goodwill and gain
Illicit and corrupt practices
trigger malice and pain

Censure not with blame game
the keenly desired selection
Harvest success or failure
the result of every action

Duty

Execute what needs to be done
carefree of the ensuing result
Duty must be rightly performed
whether it is peace or tumult

When circumstances compel
to take up even a perilous work
The committed sincerely propels
knowing it improves the world

Viewpoint

Escaping from failures
an unbecoming reprieve
regroup all the energies
for success, to achieve

Cheats

In business affairs
vigilance is required
on connecting links

The *soi-disant* friends,
mere acquaintances
just some days before

Can now simply exploit
selling dreams unviable
perhaps even fake

Leading to bankruptcy,
an alarming routine
in these uncertain times

Candor

Awakening to dignity
ascends only when
the first step towards
emancipation is taken

Else, with discipline
tossed out of the window
integrity succumbs to fraud
for petty material gains

Causing long sleepless nights
turning into a nightmare to
destroy every possibility of
harmony and equanimity

To genuinely be in self-control
dwell not in illusions unaware
become vigilant of every action
watch the next step goes where

Contrast

The sagacious
having conquered
the luring temptations,
ever ready to serve,
is the commander
whose simple nod
poses confidence,
assurance and surety;
a sign of excellence

Swayed by fairy tales,
inflicted by greed
and odious speech,
the foolish remains
incarcerated by
nefarious views and
self-destructing acts;
a sign of the burden
of unfulfilled desires

Attitude

When an incident
takes place unwittingly
and ability fails
to take control completely,

Unfavorable spell maybe,
yet it is not crass
remember steadily
that *'this too shall pass'*

React not inanely
to make the situation dire
resiliently respond,
the mess will appear minor

Acumen

Biological progression
compels everyone to age
Weary ideas sensing old
reflects a mental state

> Be amply forgetful
> to overcome grievance
> Stay reminded enough
> to challenge injustice

Unbearable suffering
deceitfulness and hate
probity warrants erasure
and start on a clean slate

> Be generously oblivious
> to abandon resentment
> Retain enough memory
> and be not threatened

Cue

Learning happens
being mindfully alive
There is surely a reason
for everything in life

One should not become
oblivious to the present
Superfluously loitering
being haughtily ignorant

It helps not assuming
a senseless attitude
Requirement is to have
a responsive fortitude

Clearly perceive the purpose
be firmly inspired and aware
Life offers achievable choices
to one who is true and sincere

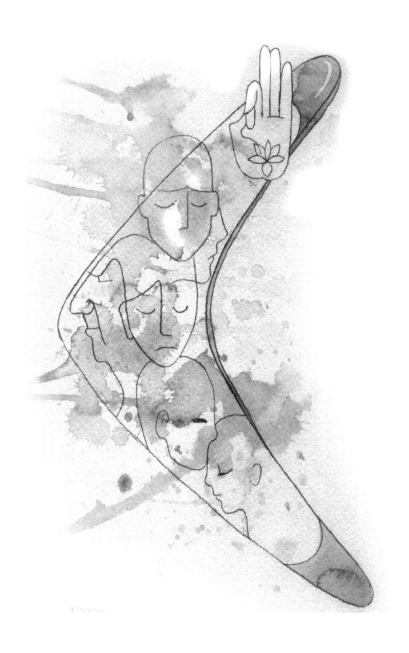

Stimulus

Instincts are inherent
react reflexively
Responses are learnt
appear thoughtfully

Anger flexes muscles
on unfulfilled desires
Calm ruminates on
cause of dissatisfaction

Fear and greed cause hate
all vulnerable impulses
Courage, contentment, love
arise from steady Self

Wisely should be chosen
the stimulus knowing
its latent potential to
aggravate or exhilarate

Greed

Enough it certainly is
to take care of everyone
strangely it is not enough
for this crazy insatiable one

Well-done

Whatever done
cannot be undone
for better or worse
may just be redone

work if being redone
should be done right
labor merits dividend
only when well-done

Approach

Unsure and uncertain
when it seems,
one needs to rationalize
the opposition between
the contradictory forces,
battling in the mind

First and foremost,
fear not the conflicts,
rather learn, how to face them
by observing the oscillations
patiently, for the real aptitude
to become apparent

Having *discovered* the talent,
without doubt, one must
earnestly pursue skillfully;
as excellence manifests in one
who is true to self than trying
to imitate or engage in a rat race.

Accord

Harmony warrants togetherness
calmness of mind
acceptance and respect
for each other's space

Cognizing perpetually
that *Life*, though forever in a flux,
is simply dynamic and wonderful,
united in its existential diversity

Ponder

The glass is hall full;
Stop tossing and turning
debating inanely, if it is
semi empty or demi full

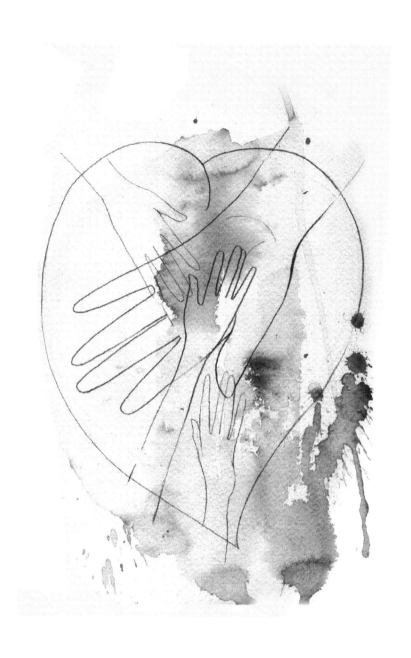

Virtue

Auspiciousness and
goodness come not
by merely wishing

Whatever comes is
entitlement of labor
bestowed by His grace

Choices

Losers, victims of lethargy,
tend to inanely settle for
existing status of poverty
and filth breeding mosquitoes

Winners too accept,
but dare with grit,
striving ceaselessly for
the basic transformation

The selection one makes
results in the life one lives
It is never too late
to make a cleaner choice

Ruling

Yes,
you were insulted
and humiliated

Surely,
you were in agony
unbearable

But
by returning *that*
in vengeance

You,
erased the advantage
behaving alike

Thus,
your right to complain
unjustified

144

Forgiveness

All along busy
blaming others for
failures self-created

Yet unwilling
even now, to learn
and extol the caring

To silence
the noise of those
haunting felonies

Better seek refuge
in the virtue of
reconciliation

Fake

Ever quizzed
the idea of sophistry
compelling one
to adorn a mask for
converting persona to
hide deceptiveness?

A person untrue
to oneself is erratic
and untrustworthy

One ought to be
simply true, for
goodness to follow

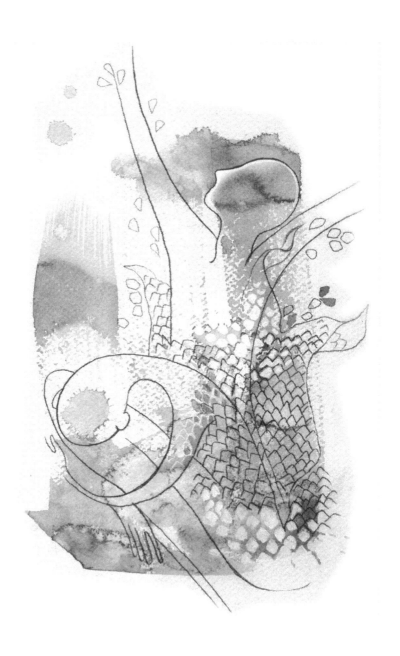

Pain

Suffering, an essential
criterion to progress!

One who does not face
trials courageously
mostly fails to become
a better person in life

Failure

There are occasions
when we meet distress
and disappointment.
Defeat seems imminent.

This too is
an effect of a cause.

When facing failure,
ask yourself, if you are
satisfied with the intent
and the effort you have put in.

The situation demands
an honest answer!

Routines

Don't think how far
the destination is
Think if you are
on the right path

> Be productive
> and not just active
> Pointless work
> breeds a chaotic life

When life starts
appearing complex
Cease analysis
Start tackling it

> Being worrisome
> leads to wearisome
> Habitual anxieties
> breed misery

Prayers are answered
Only if you know
why to pray
how to pray

Management

Whenever past bothers
Face it without remorse
Learning will happen
Whatever was, it was

No matter what today asks
Perform with confidence
Achievement will occur
Whatever is, it is

Dream of a better future
Prepare for it without fear
Vision will aspire, will inspire
Whatever will be, it will be

Commonsense

The scriptures
emphasize and insist
to realize the Self

Unequivocally, they
do not want anyone
to look in the mirror

For appeasing opinions
of those who, perhaps don't
even know themselves

I hear *Amma*'s words echoing:
Love yourself
by being true to yourself

Colleague

One, who may
listen quietly
but utterly ignore
and totally forget
what was heard,
all at the same time,
is either too shrewd
or is glum and
a dreary workmate

Loser

One, having lived
undignified throughout
now with a foot at
the edge of the grave
seriously craves
for that embrace

of the ultimate truth
before the permit
disintegrates into
memorabilia
called *tombstone*
of self-destruction

Expression

An impulse
seeking manifestation
separates from
the whispering notes
that beguile the mind
perpetually.

In its own flow
the molten instinct,
shapes into a question
or an erudite statement,
and when mingled;
perhaps forms a riddle.

Inducing the critic
to be the learner
and trace transient images
concealed within
the realms of
a blossoming poesy.

Blind Love

Hormonal visions are blurred
hence it is not *de rigueur*
for the two to be charismatic,
it is enough for one to be blind

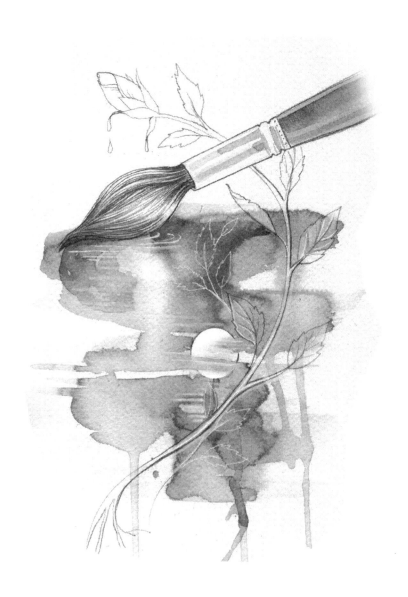

Dawn

Unveiling the darkness
Dawn projects forth
the vision of light
and the womb of silence
invigorated with her tender kiss
begins the sound of music
to wake up Life
from deep slumber
to rejoice freedom
with the fragrance of Love.

Unperturbed, the Master
paints the canvas
unifying diversity
and beating His drum
in the union of rhythms
orchestrates, the dance of the universe.

And my mind
like a droplet
rejuvenated with hope
blissfully
becomes the ocean
once again.

Desire

Love yearns to blossom
gracefully like a blooming vale
Appreciate arising inhibitions
when exploring this wondrous trail

When treading this path
be courageously honorable
With committed cause
being wisely ethical

Aver then with promising grace
enveloping two, in one embrace
Immersing in the blissful stance
to realize the momentous trance

Fire of Life

Attraction desire
Attachment touch
Passion kiss
Compatible embrace
Aflame union

Glowing
The mystic self

Embers smoke
Loneliness ego

Inextinguishable
Fire of life
Rejuvenates again!

Marriage

Wedding is not a chancy affair
like the tossing of a coin

It is a lifelong commitment,
a practice of caring and sharing,
beginning with acceptance first
adjustments next, to grow

Weathering the seasons in unison
resolving the rifts, regularly

By counting the blessings and
celebrating the sacred ritual
of awaking together gratified,
until the final curtain is drawn

Compatibility

Hysterically they argued
Furious, she threatened
to plunge into the river
roaring in seasonal spate

He sought forgiveness
She calmed down

Composure tamed anger
With togetherness reassured
they energized each other
to rediscover fulfilment

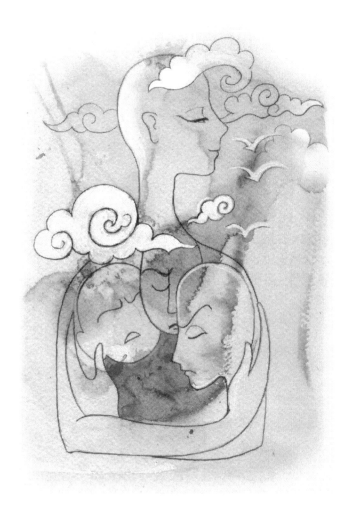

Serenity

Apprehensive, grim
anxious, provoked
before retreating
earnestly invoke
the spirit of tranquility
adorned as *Serenity*

Her arrival proclaims
a sanguine calm
initiating intimacy
with caring warmth
Serenity transforms
into a soothing charm

Undressing the *Vexed*
layer after layer
    of nefarious plots
    terrible thoughts
    panicked anxieties
    troubling worries
    brutes and monsters
    lurking in disguise
Serenity empowered
consigns the rascals
to a certain thrash
as an unwanted trash

Melodiously singing
with teasing interludes
she lovingly embraces
envelopes and engages
stroking the Vexed deep
into an unruffled sleep

Sounds simple, yet introspect
in the commotion and fanfare
Anger, malice, and protest
occur almost as a daily affair
while vital arrival of *Serenity*
is, alas, predominantly rare

Restrain thus the conflicting mind
face squarely life's daily grind
with courage, resilience, and grace
disallowing mystic *Serenity* to efface.

Togetherness

It was just the other day
if not yesterday
when we got married
forty-five* years ago

I still remember
that blessed day
when we first met
before the knot was tied

A desire arose, then,
to discover togetherness
that allows us to explore
every day, even today

*September 25, 1975

Sanctity

The sacred
consecrated bond
strengthens with
devotion

But when an
explanation is
needed, the sanctity
gets ruined

Cognition

Walking together
realization dawned
what *Life* demands

Cognition of that
got cherished as
the wondrous reward

Isn't everything else
minus that awareness
a transient trivia?

Appreciation

Passionately intense
serenely poised
expressive gestures
blissful glow

Holding book
near bosom
throbbing heart
offering thanks

Emotional ocean
ecstatic fusion
moistened eyes
love unsurpassed

Mismatched

Incompatibility
made them fight,
he walked out
feeling deluded
deserting her
years ago

Exhausted, aged
unfulfilled, jaded
and confused
now sitting in a
mountain cave, he
draws her paintings

Cursory

The infatuated innocence
raised the bar to place the beloved
on a pedestal, virtually deifying,
naming it as Unconditional Love

Until the passage of time exposed
the not godly, but all too human traits,
burdened with one's own weaknesses,
erasing the hallowed ideas

In place then appeared concepts of
pity, consolation, fate, sympathy etc.
Even a cursory exchange became
a tirade or an invective and tiring chore

Coby

A sudden vacuum sensed
an unthought-of deficiency felt
arising with absence of association
that terminated after 12 long years
with Coby – the Chocolate Labrador
who was yet another companion
in my place of work
besides other colleagues

Coby often shared and relished
breakfast and lunch with me
besides coyly nudging
for a gentle caress

I admired his intuitiveness
for he always grasped
my fatigue or boredom
and took an imposing stance

> by quietly entering my cabin
> never barking
> making circles
> wagging his tail
> twitching his eyes
> like a professor

beckoning me
to take small breaks

in all seasons
for brisk walks
or a short game of chase
in our office compound

It was an experience to note
his territorial domain
the markings of which
he sniffed and reinforced
every time during those walks
registering his freedom and
celebration of life.

Coby - our loveable Labrador
is no more ...
I cannot help but notice
moistness in my eyes.

Coby left us on September 11, 2012.

The Maple Tree

The maple tree
in our backyard
    my associate for several years
    witness to my feelings
today suddenly appeared
stern and somberly stiff

Does the autumn
    triggering the leaves
    to change
    their hue and color
    and fall one by one
    to eventually
    desert the tree
    lone and forlorn
resemble
the echo of hullabaloo
sparked by the storm
of erratic thoughts
vacillating
in my mind?

Tree of Life

Somewhere in the deep woods
I am standing blossoming with vigor
and growing in my branches
with ripening fruit
enclosing the seed of the future
awaiting that timeless moment
in the prolific season
when the seed will find itself
assimilated to sprout again
in the unfailing womb of creation.

As the tree of life
though seemingly whole
I silently persist
in clinging to earth
for sustenance and power
to realize the eternal glory
of the cycle of changing seasons.

Naissance

Listening
in silence,
the vibe rising,
echoes footsteps
of a giant oak,

directing focus on
a nascent sapling,
emerging calmly
yet resolutely,
from the soiled rocks

The glistening dew
moistens warmly
the ecstatic eyes of
an aging grandpa
on a morning stroll

Perfection

Nature
seasonal
self-controlled
orderly

In force with
each movement,
compassionately
for equilibrium

Life knows
how to celebrate
excellently
sagaciously

The masters know it
Egomaniac does not

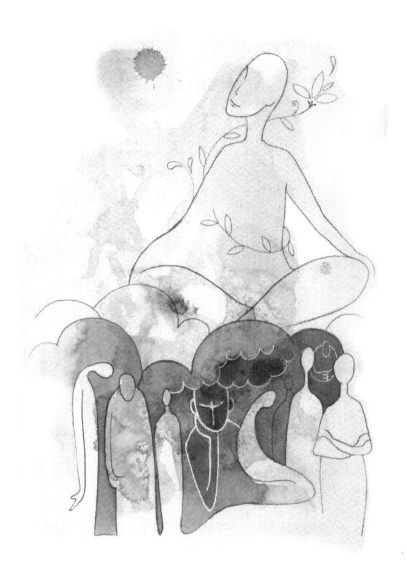

Optimist

The optimist rubs eyes
to the alarm's ringtone
on the smartphone
and not finding a tweet
or a WhatsApp message

Publicizing *the* name
in the obituary columns,
awakens with gratitude
for a new blessed day
to celebrate life.

Performs all activities
personal and vocational
by executing,
whatever is required
to be done, earnestly.

Lovingly goes to bed
ready to embrace, again,
the ultimate night,
in her amorous glory,
to attain emancipation.

Poetry

Infant in the cradle
oblivious of the strife
sucks his hallux
for poetry to thrive

        Lips are zipped
        diffidence abounds
        yet the attentive listens
        when poetic eyes sound

Endearingly loveable
ideally compatible
despite odd prongs
they versify songs

Strange

Domineering spouse
alibi of breadwinner
mixes different lentils
for mate to segregate

> Pocketing all the joys
> greedy miser is unsure
> anxieties deem life to be
> dangerously insecure

Narcissistic scholar
quoting quotable quotes
has no direct experience
clings to what was told

> Coward pessimist quitter
> relates to suicidal creed
> The brave pauses to energize
> powering response to succeed

Forgetful

Forgetful of being
accident-prone
persists to explore
the dangerous zone

Forgets not those
puzzling disorders
inadequate memory
repeating errors

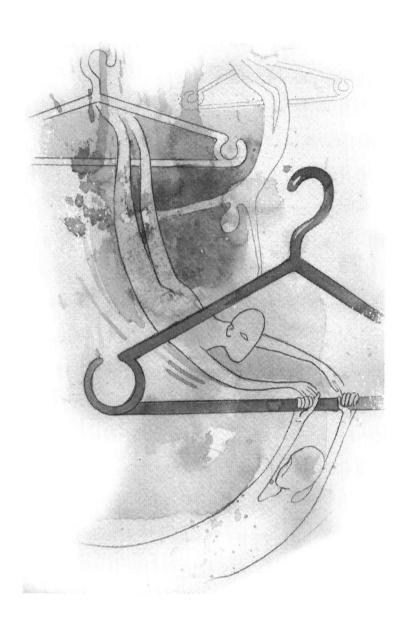

Balance

Maintaining diverse fashion
Life mystifies with passion
Scales of equilibrium necessitate
The seesaw and swing oscillate

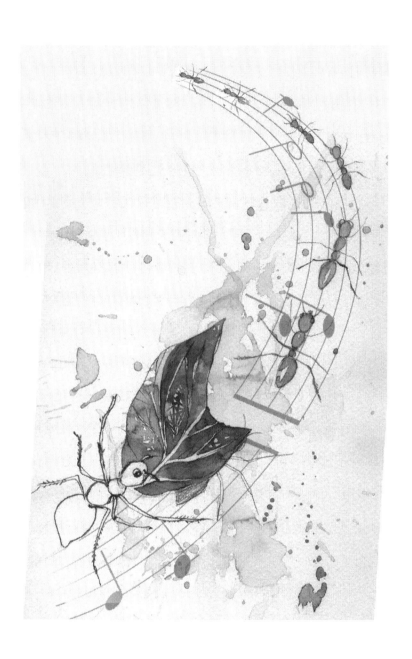

Ants

An ant in the pants;
shoe with a grain of sand
naturally disrupts
the pace of progression

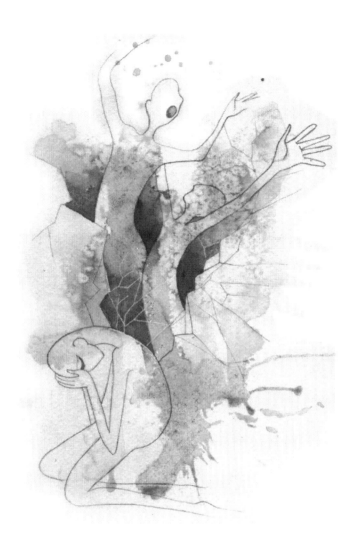

Disaster

Natural disaster strikes
several families perish
Survivors unable to wipe
tears dried on cheeks

Onus

Ordeal it is
when a loved one
struggles with the
unsought, invisible
cataclysmic visitor

Does one merely
watch helplessly?

Onus now is for
everyone to be brave
with earnest prayers
and strive to incapacitate
the catastrophic Corona

Masks

Natural beauty hidden
glamor asserts clamor
Corona-mask fashion
sets up arty designer

New Era

2020 has ushered a new era,
the invisible forces of Corona
bringing down the world to its knees

The leadership globally
appears gullible and foolish
trying to rule whimsically
without having capability
or knowledge of governance
surrounded by another
set of fools, who play
sycophant to such rulers
and lavish praises on their idiocies

And ironically, the ruthlessness
of the human hormonal prowess
is hell-bent to outsmart its own intelligence
and insult the common sense,
by breeding and adding
a quarter million new mouths
every day, notwithstanding
the infective environment and
devastation caused by the pandemic

Note: The global population is projected to increase by 82 million
during the year 2020 and reach 7.8 billion.

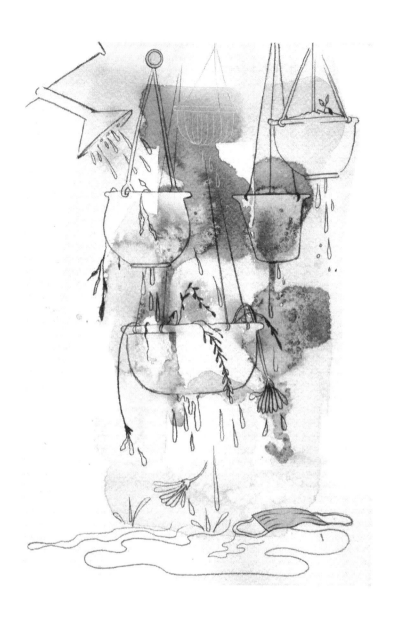

Conflicts

The levels of setback
caused by the pandemic
are not easy to fathom
and reconcile

As much as the incomes
of individuals are dwindling
so are the revenues
of the governments

Defunct
and on the verge of
becoming bankrupt
economies globally
are trying to work on
deficit financing

Who is borrowing
and who is lending
is anybody's guess!

With all social cautions
and even simple austerities
being tossed out of the window,
societies are heading
towards an environment
of mayhem and lawlessness

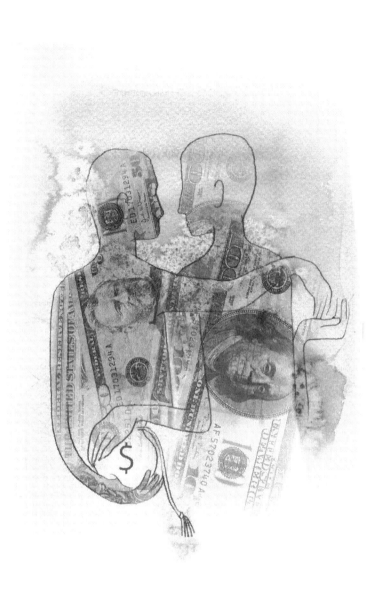

Venal

Scratching each other's back
is the new norm of camaraderie
where stupidities are tolerated
and absurdities are appreciated

Are humans being rewired to
become the masterminds who
survive by a self-deceiving mode
to earn a loaf of bread?

The deadly wave of *Corona*
seems to be aggressively distorting
social ethos and the worldview;
times are really getting tough

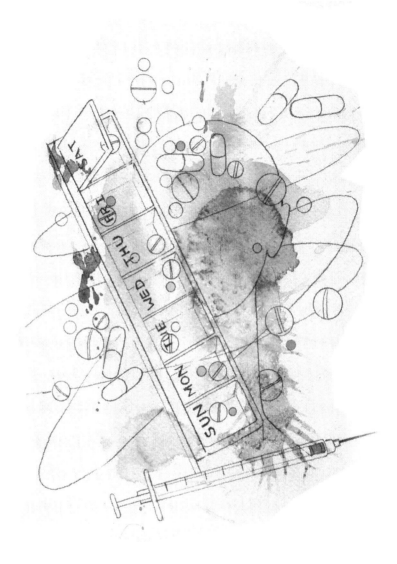

Syndrome

Today, I had my
annual physical checkup.
What all these years seemed
to be an annual ritual, now
suddenly made me realize,

That with all the marvels
of medical technology, involving
hi-tech machines, specialized doctors
and of course, branded medicines
highly marketed colorful tablets, capsules,

Some bitter and strong syrups
to be taken empty stomach
with food, before dinner,
after dinner, just before sleeping,
maintaining strict schedule

Of intervals, every day
with a plethora of other treatments
and innumerable do's and don'ts;
the fight to remain alive itself
is becoming a novel ailment

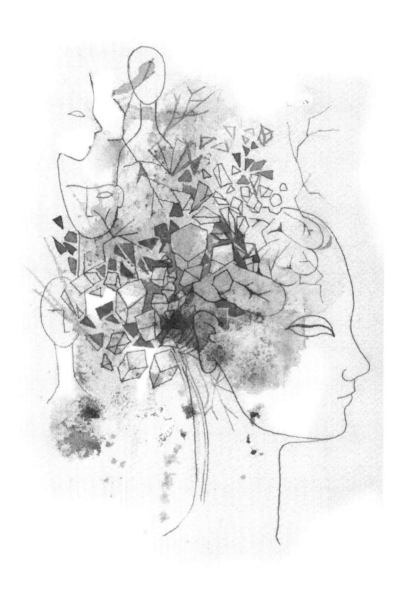

Dementia

Dementia may not be fatal
but it can be ruinous and lethal

Imagine one's impatience
manifesting as violent anger,
employed all logics, but
tossed ethics out of the window
for whatever reason
and in that maniac moment
one misbehaved
and mistreated another

And now, having carried
the burden of guilt for long,
Alas, one suffers from dementia
the disease of forgetfulness.
Thus, hallucinating
is unable to seek forgiveness
from either the other
or to exonerate one's self

Does one need to wait
to witness the irony of fate?
One should learn and follow
Yam, the *sutras* of self-control.

Encounters

Imagine walking on a path
generally wandering
In search of light
while the Sun blazes in zenith

Feeling lonely amidst a crowd
listening sounds in solitude
Being abruptly halted
to experience, out of the blue

The sudden spurt of a geyser
impulsive tornado, torrential rains
All drenching rapturously to activate
the resurgence of life cycles

With such encounters
the mesmerized wanderer continues
To explore the labyrinth of life
carefree of the destination

Carefree

Why follow a way
that makes one go astray?
Get leashed, feel secure
ramble not, so they say

Isn't this *how and why*
the perennial question
posed for millennia
generation after generation?

Was the wanderer ever tied
with instructions this way?
Bondage free then and even now
he treads carefree all the way

236

When

The question
is no longer relevant
about *why*, *how*, *where*
if one feels gratified
of having lived life
positive and content

The query does make
one not only wonder,
but also, patiently await
that ultimate moment, *when*
dissolution embarks to embrace
the majestic darkness of *Life*

Previews

Wanderer: Musings of A Mystic Poet

Wanderer is yet another significant contribution of the poet, author and entrepreneur Rajender Krishan in a quick succession after the recent release of his anthology of poems *"Amma's Gospel"* in 2020. Many of his poems often have a deep philosophical contents and spiritual nuances, and his current collection of poems is no exception.

In literal sense, a wanderer is a person that travels around extensively rather than settling at one place, often setting own rules in the process deviating from the society's norms. But here what the poet probably implies is the abstract wandering of soul over the spiritual and metaphysical aspects, people's mundane lives, the karmic cycle, and the actual purpose of life.

The present anthology is comprised of precisely hundred poems reflecting various moods and attributes of the much enlightened and mature poet, who perhaps as Wanderer goes on to exploring philosophical concepts, spirituality and aspects of mundane life, in some places as a mere observer and at others as a wise pedagogue. In the very first poem "Inexpressible", the stated philosophical nuance is clearly visible when the Wanderer says:

That what is inexpressible
is best to remain nestled
as the eternal witness...

... ...

wonderful play
of cyclic life, should it even matter
who finds whom, next?

The poet's conviction of the formless and invisible god further unfolds in the opening lines of the next verse "View", when he says...

That what is formless
is yet the only eternal form

Here obviously, the reference is to the almighty God, who is best described as Brahman in Hinduism.

A mystic is usually understood as a person who directly experiences the Supreme Being, usually unmediated by conventional religious rites and rituals, or intermediaries, transcending established belief systems and after bypassing the intellect and ego. The undulation between the Wanderer and mystic thoughts and perceptions continues through many verses exploring various aspects of spirituality.

Beyond the physical attributes of the person, the human mind is the most complex and potent abstract organ as concluded by the poet visualizes the mind as the product of the grand cosmic design accommodating all opposing perspectives. According to the Samkhya School of Hindu philosophy, the dual nature of life is on account of the two aspects of the physical reality i.e., the *Purusha* and *Prakriti*.

The *Purusha* is defined as the Self or the subject, who has awareness while *Prakriti*, on a much broader canvas, encompasses everything that is seen or known in the objective universe, including material and psychological.

The poet's in-depth spiritual knowledge and understanding as also its evocative revelation to the mundane world as expressed in the following lines of "Creativity".

The invigorated poet dives in
the ocean of fantasy to reach
its very depths to witness
the unfolding of the marvel,
from one form to another
changing from grosser
to subtler to sublime layers;

briefly, comes face to face
with what is the formless,
limitless and endless.

In between these musings, the poet remembers the role of parents and more particularly the mother in creation and continuation of life in the physical universe. His poem "Mother" presents a simile with the role and importance of the mother in creation and nurturing of her offspring akin to the similar role of the Master of Universe in creation and sustenance.

While aptly dealing with the spiritual and mundane aspects of the world and human life through umpteen verses, the poet tends to assume a higher pedestal commensurate with his wisdom and knowledge and tries to give worthy advice to the less knowledgeable and ignorant on many living aspects.

From various writings, it is amply clear that the poet has remained deeply influenced by his revered grandma whom he fondly addresses as "Amma" and considers an eternal source of inspiration and guidance.

The poet has dedicated quite a few verses on the subjects like marriage, conjugal relationship and love which are perhaps the most important aspect of the mundane and material life of the human species that most people are able to live and experience in whatever way.

With "Carefree", Rajender unwinds revealing his own mind and heart as the *Wanderer* hints of going against the flow, the usual dictum being a secured life through compliance rather than going astray, bondage free to explore the labyrinth of life without caring or bothering about the destination.

Was the wanderer ever tied
with instructions this way?
Bondage free then and even now
he treads carefree all the way.

All the poems have been further augmented by Niloufer Wadia, who has made a significant value addition to this anthology through her pictorial illustrations. I hope the Wanderer would invite a mass appeal and instant following bringing more laurel and success to the distinguished author-poet.

- Dr. Jaipal Singh
Educator, Bureaucrat, Corporate Advisor,
Lucknow

Exploring the Labyrinth of Life

Wanderer by Rajender Krishan explores the labyrinth of life's carefree poetic engagements. The sense of right and wrong pokes, nudges through poetic thoughts of Rajender. His poems leave us to think more. Some of his poems take us to a fuzzy world of *why*, *how* and *where* if one feels gratified of having lived life earnest and beaming. The questioning mind does make one not only wonder, but also, patiently wait for that poignant moment, when dissolution embarks to embrace the majestic shades and slopes of Life.

Rajender Krishan's well-crafted poems amalgamate arresting imagery with barmy, yet poetically logical, shifts in their provocatively opaque poetic space[s].

- Prof. Jaydeep Sarangi
is a fellow Indian poet, editor and professor,
and the author of *Heart Raining the Light*
anchored in Kolkata.

What the Pen of a *Ramta Jogi* or the *Wanderer* Says in 21st Century!

A *wanderer* or a *ramta jogi* is the gatherer of ideas: ideas that are rooted in the experiences of life. He is like a bird in flight: observing the world without judgement. Sitting in a living room fitted with all the possible technologies of the world, one is winged enough to wander. What come in the mind of such a 'meditative,' 'wandering,' 'warrior' of a mystic in 21st century is well-stated in the *Wanderer* of Rajender Krishan. He wonders at the enigmatic anxiety of the chaotic world. In his attempt to understand life he acknowledges the 'vagaries of the human mind': its weaknesses and its latent potential. He bows in front of the power of nature (even as malign as the Corona Virus) and finds solace in the company of a dog and a tree. As expected, his attempts leave him wiser; and the poet in him just sits and writes, accepting what is being offered, spreading the message of sanguinity. His soul is stationed like the sun and the mind reaches out, wanders: *forever a learner*. He passes all this in a style that is simple yet hard-hitting. The brevity of his expression says it all!

- Dr. Sulakshna Sharma
(aka Shelly Sharma) is a critic, editor, a reviewer and the author of *When Devil Married God: An Anthology of Stories.*

Wanderer is Absorbing

Wanderer is an absorbing, philosophical and a powerful book of poems by the master poet Rajender Krishan.

While we find ourselves helplessly tossed in the chaotic waves of the present pandemic era - the poet through his meditative contemplation is able to see through a pattern of peaceful flow of pure energy and appeals everyone to deep delve in it with his mantra 'being true to oneself'.

The unique collection of hundred poems is a soothing journey to explore our true Self by turning inwards, liberating oneself from the bondages and finally enabling us to connect to the primordial energy- ever flowing, ever nourishing and ever fulfilling.

The poems have a calming effect on the aggrieved human psyche. They are timeless and priceless pieces of jewelry, wonderfully crafted submerged in spirituality and embossed with moral and ethical values, suited for all generations.

- Neera Pradhan,
Lecturer and Counsellor, Bhubaneswar

In Appreciation of the Wanderer

The poems of Rajender Krishan strike a chord with me. His poems are a kind of personal journey for me. The simple language, the unassuming air and deep underlying philosophy endear me. There is not much scheme. There is spontaneity. There is connection to certain universal patterns.

For example, the word 'wanderer' has profound universal connotations. When Carl Jung explains the importance of universal archetypes in the functioning of the human psyche, he underlines certain universal archetypes. He interestingly discusses the cave human and how the primitive human wandered from cave to cave, from mountain to mountain and from terrain to terrain. That image, that feeling, that primitive human Wanderer is a universal archetype.

We all relive the Wanderer in our dreams. It is part and parcel of the human psyche. When 'Wanderer' fell in my hands, I was lured. I have read and reread these poems and have relished their taste.

It is not possible to circumscribe the Wanderer. The Wanderer will find his own way.

The *Wanderer* undoubtedly contains the best of Rajender Krishan. It is full of one gem after another. It is difficult to decide which poem is better than the other. It is a thinking soul's response to the experience of life. The whole realm is in the mind. It is all about thinking. It's all about perception from where life derives its meaning. The perception is uniquely philosophical. The focus never wavers. The focus is on the crux of the matter. The poet catches the essence of things.

Here are sutras, precepts, observations and conclusions based purely on the poet's encounter with life. Poems on Covid make the collection all the more contemporary and current. I enjoyed reading each word, thinking on the words served, eschewing and finding my own meanings. The collection is a treat for the literature lover. Poems flow effortlessly. Reading requires no painful effort. The reader flows easily with the poems. Reading these poems is an enriching experience.

- Prof. Shubha Tiwari,
Author /Professor and Head,
Department of English,
A.P.S. University, Rewa, M.P.

Pondering Deep
into the Psyche of a Metaphysician

The volume of verses titled *Wanderer* by Rajender Krishan, ponder deep into the psyche and the mind of a metaphysician who creates the volume as a sublime hymn. The verses delve deep into the mind of the poet and talks of his mystic diverse ideas. These hundred verses in the book talk of diversity and the wandering of the mind and consciousness of the poet. The poems impress the readers with their diverse themes and expressions of an idealist.

The poet appears to be highly disturbed by the tragedy that gripped the world due to pandemic and this volume is the cathartic outpourings of the trauma and despair caused by the deadly disease. Pandemic has changed the world. We have come to know of the transience of our lives and that we should respect our biosphere, the environment, and the atmosphere. A creative person to the core, the poet seeks several answers to his inquisitiveness which have transformed into remarkable verses.

The poet is, indeed, a wandering mystic. His mind touches from fragrance to love, to virtue, cognition, to veracity and optimism. He keeps on changing his roles, from a doting son to that of a philosopher who is knowledgeable and aware of grandeur of Indian philosophy, Samkhya, and Vedanta philosophy. The invigorated poet dives deep in the ocean of fantasy to reach its very depths to witness the unfolding of the marvel, from one form to another changing from grosser to subtler to sublime layers; briefly, comes face to face with what is the formless, limitless, and endless.

Having experienced such a transcendence, the poet aiming to articulate the infinite, ends up embracing duality, to give birth to poetry. How wonderful! And then the mystic decodes:

Meditative mystic
wants to remember
by unlearning
what was learnt (*Cipher*)

Niloufer Wadia wonderfully depicts poets' wanderings and imagination and complement his poetry with her artistic illustrations. Indeed, his thoughts from droplets become an ocean as he introspects despite the pandemic and hopes for a *New Era* and a *Dawn*.

- **Mandira Ghosh,** Author /Poet,
Treasurer, The Poetry Society (India)

Meditative Lyrics in the Post-Truth Age

The 20th century began with a note of despair in English literature. The 1st WW, the Plague (1918-20), the Great Depression (1913) and the Second WW made the world a wasteland ground. Much was lost in the turmoil, what was garnered broadly was technology – its telling effects on human affairs – relations, thought, faith, behavior, psyche etc. Today, nearly a century later, life seems to have gone beyond the boundaries of the post-modernist era, paving way for another discourse, another correlation and progression, in art and literature.

"Wanderer" is Rajender Krishan's collection of 100 poems, and it takes the reader to realms the poet may not have intended. The intentional fallacy is palpable as the poet has a definite design, intention and projection. The poet's credo is clear in his poem 'Expression':

Inducing the critic
to be the learner
and trace transient images.
concealed within.

The idea of a critic as a learner is introduced here as post modernism had liberated a critic's hegemony over the creative writer. The point is that as a critic explores, investigates and appreciates a poem, he is like a partner in the evolutionary process of critical assessment. Transient images indicate non transparency of images in poetry and that nothing is fixed, static or absolute in life and art.

The poems are predominantly written from an intellectual perspective. In a way, the poems deceptively turn the familiar unfamiliar. This is considered a virtue in poetry.

The poet is well aware of the tools of poetry. The collection displays an adept use of figures of speech. The poems, in many ways are a unique blend of knowledge and wisdom. In our post-truth age, it is through language a poet visits and re-defines his/her inherited value-systems and philosophies. This is how the poet uses poetic language to re-vision a worldview that came to him as a postmodernist legacy in times of the onslaught of globalization and technology.

There are two kinds of poets: Those that write to find out what they feel, the other to tell us what they know. Rajender falls in the latter class who instructs his readers to share and sum up the basic truths of life. Poetry to him comes as a source of inner awakening in the form of *sutras*. He catches a mood, a thought, an experience and enlarges it into a poetic image. The reader gets the feeling that he/she has understood the thought. Then it reverberates in the mind restoring the calm and poise making the reader realize that there is more to it than meets the eye. That is probably true of all real poetry – secular or spiritual.

In these hundred poems of the Wanderer, what is to be seen and appreciated is what lies at the center of the poem as we as Indians have our own cultural identity in life and culture. As an affirmation of our cultural identity, the poems are a part of post-modernist process in contemporary times, not as a historical process, but as a poetic manifesto. The poet visits tradition as change in literary taste is perpetual. The volume 'Wanderer" signifies this welcome change – a departure from the mainstream post-colonial Indian English poetry. It is direct, communicates, aphoristic with solid meditative content. 'Wanderer' is a read-must for poets in the making.

- Rajiv Khandelwal
English-Language Poet

A Beautiful Gift to Humankind

"Poetry lifts the veil from the hidden beauty of the world, and makes familiar objects be as if they were not familiar." - P.B. Shelley

A poet is an observer, a thinker, a philosopher and an interpreter. A poet not merely expresses his own ideas, but the ideas of the prevalent society, the ideals that occupy the foremost place, the philosophy of life that influences the hearts of the millions of readers and the life experiences of not only his own life but those of others as well. The poet's views are timeless and eternal which continue to influence generations and generations to come, unveiling the truth and essence of life.

Rajender Krishan is one such poet whose thoughts, ideas and philosophies shall be imbibed by the readers for ages and ages. His poetry not only focuses on the present scenario of the ever changing, drastically transforming world but his poems reflect the possibility of the influence of the ideals of truth and contentment in conquering the ego, overcoming pride and establishing inner peace and harmony in a tranquil environment.

The eternal truth and the mystifying presence of the manifested force create the surrounding aura in the mortal world and in this beautiful world, where the human being is often misled by distractions, the guiding light helps the misled soul to finally achieve the destination.

One may have all the mental knowledge in the world and yet be immature to face the vital difficulties in life. The original action of the mind accepts the evidence of the senses, the impulses and only tries to give them some direction and possible success. The experience of the mind is the controller of all actions, reactions and judgments. Mind is the dubious outer layer of conscious existence and, as the scriptures say, it needs to be tamed and conquered.

According to the philosophy of *The Bhagavad Gita*, there is only one Doer (*Karta*) of all the actions that take place in this illusory world and all the members of this world are merely actors whose reins are held by the Master Himself. During this life, the attachments are ample, and the human mind increasingly gets trapped into the labyrinth of life, which becomes the reason for discontent and disharmony of the self.

The poet warns about such illusions and presents a clear picture of the carefree untainted conscience untouched by the entangling complexities and the miseries of life.

The ego has never been easy to get rid of. Despite all the knowledge related to the ill effects and consequences of the ego on the higher planes of consciousness and the impediments it imposes in the spiritual and personal progress of the self, the human being hardly wishes to let it go. Without persistent rejection one cannot be liberated from the clutches of the ego. It is only when the limits of the ordinary self are broken, that the mind enters a wider and enlarged consciousness and the possibilities of getting rid of the ego take birth.

The poems in Rajender Krishan's book 'Wanderer' candidly and succinctly try to raise questions and answers covering the various facets of life. This is perhaps the most beautiful collection of poems I have ever read.

- **Giti Tyagi**
Academic, Author/ Poet

A Fascinating Wanderer

I know poets belong to a different clan of creative writing. They are more emotional, sensitive, vocal and, well, at times whimsical and moody also. Their expressions vary from simple and straight forward to complex and enigmatic at times. Nevertheless, they never feel tired of expressing themselves candidly most of the times.

I have been following Rajender Krishan's writing for long. He is knowledgeable, receptive and quite sensitive to the happenings around him. They trigger him from time to time to pen his thoughts short or long he prefers to share.

I was fortunate enough to read the preview of the hundred verses he had penned under the title 'Wanderer'. In the Preface itself he tells the readers the substance of the book, that 'thoughts seem to go nowhere or merely hover aimlessly'. The titles of the poems are quite simple and relatable to our daily life except a few.

I feel, most of them are unbridled expressions of what the author felt in the journey of life as a Wanderer. In general, all the hundred verses are extremely readable as well as relatable to oneself to life and its shades.

Nitpicking? Yes. Though the author's style is simple and stylish in his own way, some places they sound more prosaic or abstract. But they are very few.

In one way or other we are all 'Wanderers' unaware of our destinations. Our passages are unquestionably strewn with roses and thorns. When persons like us tread them as an exercise, a poet like Rajender Krishan could identify the nuances of them and bring them in the form of short and long limericks.

I cannot but admire the illustrations in black and white in the modern genre for each title by Niloufer Wadia. They are eye catching and thought provoking.

A book should make one think after reading it. 'Wanderer' is bound to make every reader ruminate over the life and its trail after reading these hundred poems.

- G. Swaminathan,
Chemical Engineer, Chennai.

Wander: The Philosophical and Metaphysical

While reading the text of Rajender Krishan's *Wanderer,* I was reminded of another great book of classical wisdom, *The Wanderer* by Kahlil Gibran. As I was half-way through Rajender's *Wanderer,* I felt tempted to read that book after more than a decade. Both the books shine by contrast in their own way for the one has short prose pieces as allegories and parables and convey the essence of philosophical wisdom for everyday human life; the other is a book of short poems in which the poet is grappling with the urgent confrontations, dualities of mind and spirit, intellect and the soul, in the context of bodily needs and pleasures in daily human life and quest for the Supreme since ages dealt with by the seers and sages in all literatures, even in scriptures. Some pieces of Kahlil Gibran, I would specially mention before taking up Rajender's poetic wisdom, *"The Other Wanderer", "The Quest", "The Two Poems", "The Full Moon", "Yesterday, Today and Tomorrow".* In another piece of lasting sagacity, *"The Dancer",* Kahlil Gibran says -

> *"The philosopher's soul dwells in his head, the poet's soul in his heart, the singer's soul lingers about his throat, but the soul of the dancer abides in all her body."*

259

Here in his *Wanderer*, Rajender Krishan, the "anxious wanderer" is searching for the "eternal form" in the "formless" "oblivious to the transient spectacle" (*View*). In *"Inexpressible"*, the poet says-

"In this wonderful play
of cyclic life, should it ever matter
who finds whom, next?"

If Rajender is philosophical and metaphysical in these short pieces of profound pragmatic wisdom, he is at his best in sincerely attempting to resolve the irritating, and even tortuous, dualities and confrontations. Search for remembrances and reminiscences is significant - "You and I have to be cordial for cheers!" All dualities, the conflicts of conscience, remain painful; scriptures may imprint hard to conquer mind with sharp and insightful logic and ethics; even this dynamic leaves behind doubts, shaken faith, doldrums in the spirit and even submission!

The meaning and purpose of life are actually and effectively traced in self-denial, self-discipline and self-restraint – ephemeral and the divine. Ever-active confrontation of human mind with morality, spirituality , logic and ethics to know what is right and wrong, good and bad and where to draw a line. This is the eternal obsession and dilemma with which sensitive human beings keep grappling all their life and experience no true happiness. Those who work for live and feed bodily pleasures remain unconcerned with this issue. Our consciousness of being right and doing right, doing all good and no evil troubles us more. Alexander Pope says -

"Honor and shame from no question rise,
Play well thy part, there all the honor lies."

The American National Poet, mystic and transcendentalist, and a wanderer, says -

"I have said that
the soul is not more than the body,
And I have said
that the body is not more than the soul,
And nothing, not God,
is greater to one than one's self is......."
- (*Song of Myself* by ~~Alexander Pope~~) *Walt Whitman*

The poet in Rajender Krishan experiences the transcendence to "articulate the infinite/ends up embracing duality/to give birth to poetry." (*Creativity*)

The drama of life being eternally played on world's stage with the entire creation as actors - a tribute to the rain of pleasures and "drowning agonizingly in the floods of sorrow"; it is an elusive drama, and its meaning is traced and understood in bravely fighting the battle. So, to be the performer, all seers agree and advise. (*Insight*). We are here to elevate the ephemeral and the mundane to avoid absurdity and feel the harmony in the "chaotic drama." The scholars, the philosophers, the mystics, the sufis, the sages and the seers discuss the fundamentals that disgrace and degrade life and emphasize the suppression of these flaws, common and frequent in human character, and fulfill the purpose of life to be something in nothing, says the wandering mystic, the meditative mystic, to liberate ourselves for higher destiny and wander carefree. The poet in Wanderer convinces the reader that life has to be a song of liberation to be hummed blissfully failing which it all will come to naught as a wavered discourse on death. He says -

"In the rat race, when
each one is trying to
outdo everyone else,
wanting to be the best.
The wandering mystic
continues to bask
in the pristine glory
of his unique self."   - (*Matchless*)

Thus, leave the footprints on the sands of time and the ever-dancing waves on the sea of life! The meditating mystic preaches humble gratitude and total submission to His Will as a mystic warrior staying disciplined and virtuous to gather pearls of wisdom and the bliss of the beauty of life discarding the venom of hatred and jealousy for the essence of love. Here begins the venerated self with the fragrances of love, piety and enlightenment after crushing and burying the falsehood, hypocrisy, crookedness as -

"Times are uncertain,
Life unpredictable
... ...
... ...
The new journey
must begin unsullied,
without any luggage,
to explore the unknown." - (*Wanderer*)

In this context, "*Schooling*" is the best lesson of faith, wisdom, hope, harmony, vibrant and dynamic forward movement on the paths of life to fresh glory. Teacher-student interaction is unending and ever-ceaseless beyond, consciously or unconsciously- all goes unawares then! Here it leads to the fine discovery of Thine and Mine, explaining the cause and effect, Karma yoga, the reward or award of what we give or do, what we cultivate here and there and everywhere. All false presumptions must be shed in all honesty to seek and reach beyond! Cheats and frauds, exploitative tendencies to loot and plunder shall dim the light and obstruct the vision and lead astray into the blind alleys- so where to reach and when to reach

263

the destination? Self-control and self-denial to destroy illusions, deceit, greed, odious thoughts and designs, shall carve a smooth course to emancipation- our submissively declared goal to sustain Life's "existential diversity". Not mere wishes but His Grace alone showers this blessing. The Wanderer stops not, nowhere; the mystic wanderer has honestly realized that sufferings and pains and miseries endured with an ungrudging sense of submission and reconciliation shall quicken the pace of dynamic growth and advancement. Prayers are certainly answered - is the unflinching faith of the wanderer. Fulfillment of the dreams and passions of life is assured in continuous pursuit. Here again, the poet remembers Amma's gospel and stands reassured that this is the essence of scriptures. These are the beautiful "realms of a blossoming poesy" so artistically, simply, spontaneously, cryptically and rhythmically created in these short pieces by the Wanderer!

The wanderer moves on into the New Era of 2020, New Normal created, imposed and forced by the proponents of pandemic upsetting and devastating the global pattern of political, economic and social life causing severe damage to the deteriorating physical and psychological human behavior. The poet's serious and genuine concern is obvious in his indictment and denunciation of the way New Era is being understood, handled and guided by the idiots, stupid, wiseacres, fools and sycophants. He has the dare to say -

"The leadership globally
appears gullible and foolish
trying to rule whimsically
without having capability
or knowledge of governance
surrounded by another
set of fools, who play
sycophant to such rulers
and lavish praises on their idiocies." - (*New Era*)

This is "the infective environment and /devastation caused by the pandemic" resulting in global economic ruin by the prophets of depopulating the world -

"where stupidities are tolerated
And absurdities are appreciated." - (*Venal*)

Amidst this is being practiced the pharmaceutical chaos and loot causing serious disturbances in human behavior like dementia, violent anger, mania, hallucination etc. The poet declares with an unanswerable question -

"Was the wanderer ever tied
with instructions this way?
Bondage free then and even now
he treads carefree all the way." - (*Carefree*)

Perhaps, the wanderer suggests that there is a clear revolt against the autocratic impositions of the governance at all levels. This is "the majestic darkness of *Life*" and the wanderer has to wait patiently for "that ultimate moment."

Here is an ageless wanderer with the ageless quest for the ageless wisdom to liberate human mind of its ageless dilemma and confrontations and illumine and brighten the course life for a *New Destiny* in human history!

Hopefully, this book of Rajender Krishan is well-received by the poetry lovers and general readers everywhere!

Best of reading!

- Prof. R. K. Bhushan Sabharwal
Academic, Poet, Author, Critic, Ludhiana.

Humane Vibes in Wanderer

Humane vibes are conspicuous standpoints that define poet's eclectic feelings contained in poetry book: *Wanderer* written by noted poet-- Rajender Krishan. Poet has adopted free verse style dispensing with regular rhythm and rhyme. Poems are suffused with creative image motifs that pinpoint varying human traits, such as, deceit, hypocrisy, apathy and many agonizing experiences of the poet.

Being of a linguistics expertise, I am moved to explicate the foregrounding of subtle shadings of feelings of the poet apparent in a lot of poems. In so many poems, the poet has exercised *personification*.

By way of subtle use of poetic device – **ellipsis** apparent in the deliberate omission of essential subjects (shown through three dots…), semi-sentences are embedded in the poem: "*Transformation*":

…"went to the temple
to get some peace
…came back lugging
the tightened identity
of a burdened typecast
…Bumped into a mystic

discussed a prosaic idea
...returned home
with a fractured ego
but a liberated Self."

Adjectival phrase – **fractured ego** implies personification in the sense that abstract noun "ego" is collocated with concrete human attribute adjective – *fractured*. It is obvious in the poem that wanderer acquires liberation only when he scans himself and shuns trivial ideas.

In the poem *"Contentment"* humane virtues are perceived in the prime persona – **wanderer:**

"the wandering mystic urged,
Forbearance and patience, instead of
wickedness and anger
suggested goodwill and
harmony, in place of
venom of hate and envy..."

In the beautiful poem: **Wanderer** quoted verbatim, a lot of significant ideational points are explicitly presented by the wanderer for becoming one with his true self:

"Times are uncertain
Life unpredictable

yet, desires abound
Seeking fulfillment.

Allow me to exert
for one more day
in my attempt to empty
the trunk of cravings

The new journey
Must begin, unsullied,
Without any luggage,
To explore the unknown.

Verily all will belong
To the same Cosmos
Yet let me not wonder
as to who will meet,

walk and wander with me
on the new voyage, instead
I pray, keep me blessed
to be true to myself."

The above underscored stanzas of the signature poem – *Wanderer* bear nuanced feelings. Adjectival phrase – **the trunk of cravings** flashes personification of multiple ambitions to be concretized anyway. The underscored stanza specifying- "*the new journey...unsullied, without any luggage....the unknown*" - implies that realization of God demands flawless life. Luggage connotes load of desires. Poet's poetic craft reveals that wonderful poems can be composed without regular rhyme, rhythm and intricate figurative language.

The poet prefers humane attitude to live clean and meritorious life for the benefit of others also as reflected in the poem: "*Schooling*":

"Life taught me, incredibly young
Through accidents and *design*
How-to walk, in *sync* with *her*
Her simply tough tutoring
In the School of Challenges
Began lessons with gratitude

Followed by aptitude, fortitude,
Encouraging to aim for altitude
Smiling with a caring attitude....

Having a sincere purpose in pursuits
Being morally gratified of actions
Having humility to respect my mentors.

It is noteworthy here that the multitude of words bearing – *tude* in their end contribute to eye rhyme and internal rhyme. The word – *design* connotes ulterior motive and *sync* is an informal expression for synchronize. The other word – *her* implies life itself. The poet has explored typical upheavals that human beings have had to face in life, and he has defined good ways how-to-live an exemplary life.

In the beautiful poem: "*Marriage*", the poet has dictated excellent precepts which modern people scarcely follow:

"Wedding is not a chancy affair
Like the tossing of a coin
It is a lifelong commitment
A practice of caring and sharing
Weathering the seasons in unison
Resolving the rifts regularly
By counting the blessings and
Celebrating the sacred ritual
Of awaking together gratified
Until the final curtain is drawn."

Genuine and graceful precepts reveal that the married life can be lived peacefully and lovingly if the couple removes differences through meaningful discourse. Present participle – *weathering* implies combined efforts for sweet living by means of caring each other and sharing pains and pleasures comfortably. The phrase – *final curtain* connotes twofold meaning: divorce and death.

How tranquility and serene living can be achieved is revealed in the beautiful poem – "*Serenity*":

"Serenity transforms
into a soothing charm
undressing *the Vexed*
layer after layer
of nefarious plots
terrible thoughts
panicked anxieties
troubling worries
brutes and monsters
lurking in disguise."

In a nutshell, we can enjoy serene life only when shun the company of notorious persons who disturb us in the guise of fake friends.

To sum up the facts, it is stressed that beautiful drawings in consonance with the themes of poems enhance effectiveness of the poetry collection.

- Prof. Dr. Nar Deo Sharma
Poet, Critic, Linguist and Teacher, Noida

Wanderer Leads to
Discovery of Existential Truths

The title 'Wanderers' instantly flashes thoughts of William Wordsworth's immortal lines- 'I wandered lonely as a cloud....' referring to the wandering without a purpose until the poet spies 'a host of daffodils.' Although the wanderings of poet Rajender Krishan appear to begin aimlessly 'with a churning of fleeting thoughts,' it primarily aims to 'ascertain the destination;' in Wordsworthian language, to feel that 'bliss of solitude.'

'Wanderer,' which is also the title of this marvelous poetic collection talks about the uncertainties and unpredictable nature of human existence.... this poem is topical and relevant in today's scenario when the deadly pandemic continues to threaten the very existence of Man. Acceptance of the new norm and lifestyle modifications continues to be the therapeutic *sine qua non;* moreover, the poet earnestly desires to 'empty the trunk of cravings,' and begin the journey 'unsullied.' 'Walk and wander with me on the new voyage' is the message conveyed that implies that 'Change is the only constant' as expounded by Heraclitus, the Greek philosopher.

Rajender Krishan, is a staunch believer of freedom of expression and truth is evident in the poems that are filled with sensitivity, truth, openness, and rationality, besides offering comfort and peace. Additionally, the artistic sketches by renowned artist Niloufer Wadia are aesthetically appealing – the illustrator has brilliantly reflected the poet's thoughts precisely in images.

The poems in this collection have earnestly attempted to 'reign the wild horses galloping in the mind's racecourse' in the turbulent times we live in; accept and adapt to the 'new normal' in the best possible manner with confidence and courage. The thoughts expressed in this poetic collection will enable earnest seekers of truth to find answers to some of their own existential truths in the chaotic world around us, and leave them invigorated, resilient and blissful.

- Hema Ravi
Academic, Author, Poet, Chennai

About the Poet

Born in 1951, Rajender Krishan (*aka* Raj Chowdhry), the editor of Boloji. A graduate from Delhi University. He has extensive experience in poultry farming, advertising, sales and marketing, antique reproductions and real estate consultancy. In 1989, he migrated to New York, USA with his wife Meera Chowdhry and two children.

Rajender Krishan believes in the freedom of expression and is an admirer of *Kabir*. He is passionate about Poetry, Photography and Visual Art.

Other books by Rajender Krishan: